MW01506192

HOT LINE

Envy

by Laurie Beckelman

Series Consultant
John Livingstone, M.D.

Crestwood House
Parsippany, New Jersey

J 152.4
B ec
12-95

For Brian, Toby, and Ian

Author's Note: Many teenagers generously shared their thoughts and experiences with me. The quotes in this book are based on their stories.

Published by Crestwood House, an imprint of Silver Burdett Press.
A Simon & Schuster Company
299 Jefferson Road, Parsippany, NJ 07054

First Edition

Design: Lynda Fishbourne, Hemenway Design Associates
Packaging: Prentice Associates Inc.
Photos:
Superstock: (Charles Orrico)Cover, 26, 28, 31, 44, 46,
PhotoEdit (Richard Hutchings)4,(Tony Freeman)11, (Steve Skjold)19,
(Myrleen Ferguson Cate)20,(David Young-Wolff)23, 40, (Phil McCarten)33,
Image Bank: 9, 15, 42.

Printed in the United States of America
10 9 8 7 6 5 4 3 2 1

Library of Congress Cataloging-in-Publication data

Beckelman, Laurie.
    Envy / by Laurie Beckelman. — 1st ed.
        p. cm. — (Hotline)
    Includes bibliographical references and index.
    ISBN 0-89686-846-1   ISBN 0-382-24957-7 pbk.
    1. Envy—Juvenile literature. [1. Envy.] I. Title.
II. Series: Hotline (Crestwood House)
BF575.E6B43 1995
152.4—dc20   94-29744

Summary: A discussion of envy and how it affects relationships and self-esteem. Provides examples of typical ways in which teens express envy and offers suggestions for managing envy more effectively.

HOT LINE

Envy

C O N T E N T S

My best friend, Maria, got accepted to this special art class. At first I was really happy for her. But then I started feeling kind of sad—not for her, but for me.

It's Not Fair!

Pam: "My sister always gets more. More clothes, more dates, more friends. Even her Christmas stocking is bigger than mine! It's not fair! I hate her."

Gerald: "Roger's such a jerk. Ever since he got his new skates, he thinks he's so cool. He skates everywhere — even to baseball practice! Doesn't he know that he looks like an idiot?"

Carmen: "My best friend, Maria? Well, she got accepted to this special art class. She's really happy 'cause she loves drawing. At first I was really happy for her, too. But then, I don't know, I started feeling kind of sad. You know, not for her but for me. But it made me think about special things *I* can do."

They may not realize it, but Pam, Gerald, and Carmen all feel **envy**. Envy is the uncomfortable feeling of wanting what someone else has so badly that it hurts. Pam thinks her parents favor her sister. She envies the attention her sister gets at home and from friends. She covers her envy, and her own needy feelings, with hate. Gerald envies Roger's in-line skates. He covers his envy by putting Roger down, but if Gerald had a new pair of skates, he'd be skating everywhere, too. Carmen envies Maria's talent and the special attention and opportunities it brings. She lets herself feel sad, but then she takes care of herself by thinking about her own special talents.

Envy is a normal feeling that everybody has. We usually envy things we believe we deserve or need but will never get. We might envy someone's relationships, success, possessions, sense of humor, talent, beauty, intelligence, or popularity. Sometimes envy hurts so badly that we want to destroy what the other person has. For example, Marsha envied Claire, one of the most popular girls in her class. She wished she could make friends as easily as Claire did. Sometimes she thought, "If I had a great figure and great hair like Claire, I'd be popular, too." When Claire was in a car accident, Marsha actually felt glad for a moment. She imagined that the accident would ruin Claire's looks and make her less popular. Marsha felt guilty for having such negative thoughts. She went out and bought Claire a get-well card.

Marsha's shame at having felt envy, like her envy itself, is a normal feeling. We learn from an early age that envy is "bad." In fairy tales and other stories, envious people are ugly and mean-spirited. They act on their envy. They don't just feel it. Bad things often happen to them as a result. After all, Cinderella's stepsisters aren't the ones who get the prince. And think about Snow White's evil stepmother! She goes so far as to try to kill Snow White, whose beauty she envies. But the stepmother, not Snow White, dies in the end. And these tales aren't the only age-old warnings against envy. Envy was considered one of the seven deadly sins!

No wonder many people learn to ignore or deny envy. Allison is typical of many when she says, "I don't feel envy. It isn't nice. I think we should all be happy with what we have." But we're not all happy with what we have or who we are. And like it or not, we all do feel envy at one time or another. This feeling is neither good nor bad. It's what we do with our envy that matters.

Envy can either illuminate or cloud our lives. Like a fast-moving storm, it can pass quickly over our relationships, leaving sunshine in its wake. Carmen, for example, felt the clouds of envy roll in when she was "a little sad" after learning of Maria's success. But once she began thinking about her own talents, the cloud lifted. She began focusing on her own strengths so that she could get for herself what she envied about Maria (a special opportunity). She was aware of her envy and used it as a positive guide.

The clouds of envy can linger, however. Envy can cast a blanket of dissatisfaction over life. Like Pam, the envier may feel that he or she *never* gets enough, that nothing is fair. Envy can consume the envier. It can poison life, making what one has taste bitter because it is not the same as or as much as or as good as or as new as or as big as or as pretty as what someone else has. It is this poisonous envy that we are warned against.

You can deny or ignore envy, but this will not keep it from turning poisonous. In fact, the opposite is true. Envy is a mushroom of an emotion. It grows in darkness. If you do not recognize and address your envy, it can affect your behavior without your knowing it. And that can hurt others and yourself. But if you bring envy out into the light, it becomes yours to control. You can manage it rather than letting it manage you. The more you allow yourself to be aware of your envious feelings, the less likely you are to behave in envious ways.

This book is all about envy: what it is, what causes it, and how you can use it as a teacher. You might want to get a pen and paper before you read further. The "Take Charge!" chapters of the book have exercises that can help you recognize, understand, and better use your envy. Do them as you read the book, and by the time you're done you'll know more about your feelings and how you can make envy a positive, growth-promoting force in your life!

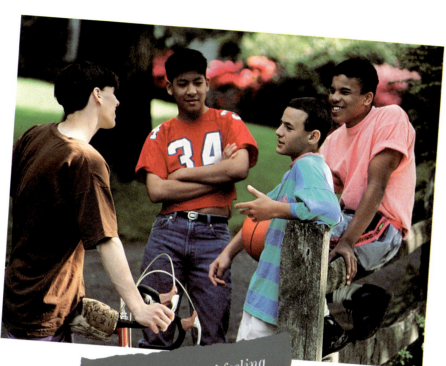

Envy is a normal feeling
that everybody has. We
might envy someone's
relationships, success,
possessions, sense of
humor, talent, beauty,
intelligence, or popularity.

Why Do People Envy?

Tony feels a slow burn whenever he sees Kevin talking to Melissa. It's not that he knows Melissa or even wants her to be his girlfriend. But he would like to be able to talk to girls as easily as Kevin talks to Melissa. "If it weren't for guys like Kevin, guys like me would have more of a chance," says Tony. "You can tell just by looking at him that Kevin's the type who gets whatever he wants. He's just like my brother, Garrett, who can get my mother to give him anything."

Of course, Kevin isn't the real reason Tony doesn't have an easy time talking with girls. Maybe Tony is shy by nature. He might need to push himself harder to feel comfortable talking with girls. Or perhaps his interests are so different from those of the girls he knows that he finds they have little in common. But in Tony's mind, Kevin is a wall separating him from Melissa and the other girls. He envies Kevin because of this.

Tony feels a slow burn whenever he sees Kevin talking to Melissa. It's not that he knows Melissa or even wants her to be his girlfriend. But he would like to be able to talk to girls as easily as Kevin talks to Melissa.

11

As is usually the case, Tony's envy reflects his perception of the situation, not the reality. A lifetime of experiences influences what we envy and why. No one grows up being able to do everything well or getting everything he or she wants all the time. We all feel deprived sometimes. Just think of how a hungry baby wails while his or her mother warms a bottle or finishes a telephone conversation! This feeling of deprivation is one of four parts of envy, writes **psychiatrist** Willard Gaylin. Comparison, powerlessness, and competition are the others. We feel envy when

- we feel deprived of something we think we deserve;
- we compare ourselves with someone who has what we want;
- we feel powerless to change the situation;
- we believe that we can't have what we want as long as the other person has it.

According to many theorists, envy has its roots in early childhood. The **analyst** Melanie Klein believed that even infants feel envy. She theorized that infants envy their mothers' ability to give food. Although not everyone agrees with Klein, most people who study child development think envy does begin early. A young boy may envy the love his mother gives his father. A young girl may envy the love her mother gets from her dad. And once brothers and sisters enter the picture, watch out!

Sibling rivalry is the term used to describe the very

natural and normal envy between brothers and sisters. Even parents who love their children equally have only so much time and attention to give. Siblings compete for their parents' attention. They compete for the last cookie, the front seat in the car, the first hug when Mom gets home from work, the most praise. When one sibling believes that another has "won" this competition, he or she naturally feels envy. If this child feels that his brother or sister *always* wins, envy can become a way of life.

Of course, some parents really do favor one child over another. And some children, with or without siblings, truly are deprived. Their parents or other caretakers may be unable to meet their needs for any number of reasons, including illness; drug abuse; alcoholism; or stress due to a job or job loss, poverty, or family problems.

The envy experienced in early relationships carries over into later life. It is like a fun-house mirror, distorting our view of current events. Tony's envy of Kevin is an example. Kevin reminds Tony of Garrett, the brother who can "get my mother to give him anything." Tony sees Kevin as stealing the attention he wants from girls, just as he sees Garrett as stealing the attention he wants from their mother. But is this true? Is Kevin, or Garrett for that matter, really in Tony's way? Or is something else going on?

Claiming Your Disowned Self

Tony grew up hearing that he was quiet and serious and a "good boy." These were the labels that adults always used to describe him. His brother, Garrett, was "the wild one," the "lady-killer," the "hot ticket." Tony got lots of praise for being quiet, polite, and thoughtful. Garrett got lots of attention and laughs for his clowning and kidding around. It was as if Tony and Garrett each had a role to play in the family; they played their roles well.

These roles grew out of their **temperaments.** Tony is by nature quieter than Garrett, and Garrett is by nature outgoing. But that doesn't mean that Tony doesn't have an outgoing side. It doesn't mean that Garrett can't be quiet and thoughtful. But Tony and Garrett's parents picked up on one son's shier nature and the other's more outgoing ways. They labeled their boys, praising seriousness in Tony and playfulness in Garrett. As a result, Tony buried the parts of himself that are like Garrett and built up his quiet, thoughtful side. This enabled him to meet his mother's expectations and thus feel secure in her love. Garrett did just the opposite. He buried the parts of himself that were most like Tony.

Everyone does what Garrett and Tony have done. We learn early in life which parts of ourselves get us the attention we need to feel safe and loved. Those parts become our **primary selves,** according to **psychologists** Hal and Sidra Stone. The parts of ourselves that we bury become our **disowned selves**.

Tony buried the parts of himself that are like his outgoing brother, Garrett, and built up his quiet, thoughtful side. This enabled him to meet his mother's expectations and thus feel secure in her love.

Our primary selves are very valuable and helpful in childhood. But as life changes and gives us new challenges, the primary selves do not always work as well as they once did, as Tony discovered. His quiet, thoughtful primary self didn't seem to help him attract girls. He envied the breezy manner that worked for Garrett and Kevin. He did not realize that he too has what it takes to attract girls. But he does!

Tony can learn to recognize his disowned outgoing self and not bury it as he has in the past to cope with living with his parents. Once he does, he will be able to tap its energy. This does not mean that he will — or should — become just like Garrett or Kevin. He's Tony, and Tony's great! In fact, Garrett envies some things about Tony. But if Tony can become aware of his disowned outgoing self, he can choose how and when to use it.

Being aware of his disowned self gives Tony choices. And the ability to choose gives him power. When we feel more powerful in our lives, we are less insecure. We have less reason to envy because we can now access those things we have envied in others.

Take Charge!
Know Your Disowned Self

We often envy in others traits that we have buried in ourselves. Our envy is like a mirror that reveals these disowned parts of ourselves. By looking into the mirror of envy, we become aware of our disowned selves. And once we are aware, we can choose to make the disowned selves part of our lives. Now this isn't easy. The disowned parts of ourselves are buried deep. Often, we so fear being rejected if we let them out that we can't acknowledge that they're there.

One good way to get around your internal censor is to write or draw what you feel. Try keeping a "Me, Myself, and I" journal. Think about someone you envy and why. What does that person have or do that you wish you had or could do? What might your wishes tell you about a disowned part of yourself?

If you can identify a disowned self, try to think of a time when you let part of it out. Can you think of a time when you acted like the

17

person you envy, for example? Write about how you felt and what happened. Or draw a picture.

Now think of a time when you wished you'd acted like the envied person but couldn't. What was different about the two situations? For example, Tony once met a girl at a party his mother's friends gave. He had no trouble talking to her. Only the girls at school seemed to be a problem. Tony might think about why he can't tap his outgoing side at school but could with the girl at the party. Are the girls different? Does he think the kids at school expect him to be quiet, just as his mother does? Does he therefore act in a way that meets their expectations? Might he need a more relaxed setting, such as a party, to let his outgoing side shine through? Questions like these can help Tony understand why he buries his outgoing side and how he might be able to let it through.

Welcoming a disowned self back into your life can be exciting. It is also difficult and risky because it means breaking old habits and changing old ideas about who you are. But if you can reclaim a disowned self, you can explore parts of yourself that might help you meet challenges in your current life. If you are aware that you are experimenting, you can see what works and what doesn't. You can begin the life-long process of choosing the "you" you want to be.

The disowned parts of ourselves are buried deep. Often, we so fear being rejected if we let them out that we can't acknowledge that they're there.

Tina's always coming to school with some new hairdo. I'm much prettier than she is, or at least I would be if I could do my hair like she does hers.

If Only I Were More Like . . .

Tasha, like Tony, has a bad case of envy. "Tina's parents have money," says Tasha, "so she goes to the beauty parlor all the time. She's always coming to school with some new hairdo. One week it's a perm. The next she's got this really cool weave. And she's not even pretty. I'm much prettier than she is, or at least I would be if I could do my hair like she does hers. *I* should be the one with money to spend on great hair."

As Tony's and Tasha's stories suggest, we envy in others what we feel is lacking in ourselves. The things we envy will, we believe, get us something we badly want. Tony thinks having a breezy, carefree manner is the key to attracting girls. Tasha thinks great hair is the key to looking pretty.

We do not come to these beliefs all on our own. Our family, **culture**, and **peer group** influence our ideas. If Tasha's friends all believe that a person has to have a perm to look pretty, Tasha is more likely to hold this belief, too. Tasha and her friends may also believe that looking pretty is the key to being popular and that being popular is the key to finding love. The movies and television programs and commercials Tasha sees reinforce this idea. The girl with the great looks always gets the guy.

Tony's mother always calls him "my serious one." She calls his brother Garrett "my lady-killer." Tony has grown up believing that you need a personality like Garrett's to attract girls. Once again, our culture reinforces this belief. On TV and in film, the guy with the quick line always gets the girl. No wonder Tony wishes he were more like Kevin or Garrett!

Ads feed our envy, too. They suggest that not only the right traits but also the right possessions are the key to success and love. Too often, we believe them. We buy the new sneakers, the new soda, or the new jeans because we hope they will get us the love and recognition we want. And if we can't buy them, we envy those who can. Some kids go to enormous lengths to get the things they envy. Some may even steal for them.

The need to feel loved and valued is often at the root of envy, points out psychiatrist John Livingstone. "What we envy is a symbol," he says. "We believe it will bring us love, recognition, relationships, respect, and a feeling of safety and belonging. We imagine that the other person has this love and security *because* he or she has what we envy. This is rarely true." What is true is that everyone feels unloved and unsafe sometimes. Everyone feels vulnerable. As a result, everyone feels envy. Developing the best of who we are and what we can do is the route to belonging and love.

Everyone feels vulnerable sometimes. As a result, everyone feels envy. Developing the best of who we are and what we can do is the route to belonging and love.

Take Charge!
Peek Beneath Your Envy

What do the things that *you* envy symbolize? To find out, take a few minutes to dream. Think of the person you most want to be like. Ask yourself, "What does that person have that I want?" Imagine having what you envy. What would it mean to you? How would your life change? Now capture your thoughts in an "envygram," a picture of your envy.

1. Draw a circle on the side of a piece of paper.

2. Write what you envy in the middle of the circle. You might write: blonde hair, muscles, or Jenny's new CD player, for example.

3. Draw a line out from the main circle. At the end of the line, write one thing you think would change if you had what you envy. Draw a circle around it. For example, you might write "More friends."

4. Think of other things that might change. Add them to the diagram in the same way.

5. Would having any of these things (more

friends, for example) bring other changes? If so, add another circle to your diagram. For example, if you thought that having more friends would mean that you'd never be bored, draw a line from "More Friends," write "Never bored" at the end of the line, and circle it. If never being bored means having a rich and happy life, add another circle to your envygram. Keep going until you run out of ideas.

Look at your finished envygram. What does it tell you? You might notice that having blonde hair or muscles or a new CD player isn't really what's important to you. Making more friends, being bored less of the time, or feeling satisfied and happy is. You might even notice that having what you envy isn't the key to getting what you want. After all, is blonde hair really the cure-all for boredom? If not, what is the route to getting what you want? What can you do with who *you* are and what *you* have to be less bored or make more friends or fill whatever need your envygram revealed? These are the important questions. And the answers lie within you. As you get to know yourself — your interests, your talents, the type of people you like — you'll begin to sense what activities and friends will help take care of the worries and wishes beneath your envy.

Allison says she never feels envy. But if she loses a race, she "hates" the person who wins. She always finds some reason to criticize the winner.

The Feeling with a Thousand Faces

Envy is a good teacher. But it can teach us only when we recognize it in our lives. Because envy is such an uncomfortable feeling, we often hide it from ourselves. Allison, for one, says she's never envious. But listen to how she talks about her competitiveness: "I go out for track. I admire winners, and I'll do almost anything to win," she says. "Once I almost bumped this girl I was racing against 'cause it looked like she was going to gain on me. I mean, it was *my* race. I deserved to win." Allison says she didn't bump into the other runner because she quickly regained the lead herself, not because bumping her would have been wrong.

Allison won that race. But when she loses, she "hates" the person who wins. She always finds some reason to criticize the winner. Often she thinks the winner didn't really deserve first place. Maybe the winner started racing before the whistle. Or maybe she had top-of-the-line running shoes, which gave her an unfair advantage in Allison's eyes. And what if one of Allison's friends beats her at something? "My friends know better than that," answers Allison quickly. "I mean, if they go up against me, they're not my friends, are they?" Even when Allison keeps some of her attitudes secret, they show in her face, her body language, and her tone of voice. She does not get the respect and acceptance she hopes winning will secure for her.

Allison's story shows many of the faces of envy. Competition, spoiling, and faultfinding are among them. Here is an explanation of these and other masks that envy commonly wears.

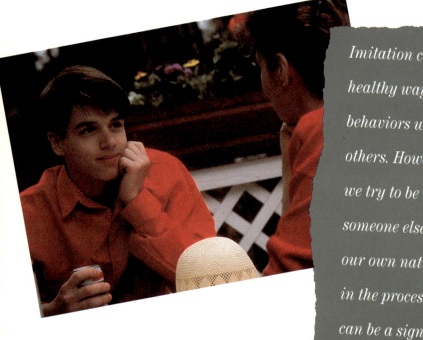

Imitation can be a healthy way to try behaviors we admire in others. However, when we try to be exactly like someone else and deny our own natural selves in the process, copying can be a sign of envy.

■ *Copying:* Imitation can be a healthy way to try behaviors we admire in others. However, when we try to be exactly like someone else and deny our own natural selves in the process, copying can be a sign of envy. Without realizing it, we may believe that if we can look like, talk like, and walk like the person we envy, we can have all the privileges we think he or she has. This is different from claiming a disowned self. People who copy haven't found a personal way of expressing the traits they envy. They are trying to be the other person. Their behavior looks and feels fake to others.

■ *Denial:* Sometimes we avoid the discomfort of envy by pretending that we don't really want what we envy. We may give up dreams or plans we had for ourselves to avoid feeling our envy. We may dismiss our wants, saying, "I don't care." "Who needs that?" "That's disgusting!" For example, Jake and Peter were both saving for new bikes when Jake's grandparents bought him an expensive mountain bike. Peter could never buy that kind of bike for himself. Rather than continuing to save for a bike he could afford, Peter spent his money on his second priority, a new video-game system that Jake didn't have.

■ *Gossip and teasing:* Spreading rumors about someone or teasing him or her are both ways of putting a person down. Doing this to someone we envy may make us feel more powerful than him or her for a moment, but the feeling rarely lasts. Making someone else small doesn't make us big.

■ *Faultfinding:* Criticizing or minimizing someone else's accomplishments is another way of putting the envied person down. Kira showed her best friend, Sue, the new dress she bought for the school dance. Sue, who wasn't able to buy a new dress, commented: "You got white? Kira, that's not a great color. That dress will be a mess! Besides, it will make you look big."

■*Spoiling:* Some people have the attitude, "If I can't have it, no one can." They express their envy by trying to spoil other people's chances of getting what they want. Whenever Damien got interested in a new girl, his friend José would tell him all the bad things he had heard about her. José didn't know whether these stories were true, but he did know the effect they would have: Damien would lose interest in the girl. He wouldn't get what José wanted for himself — a girlfriend.

■ *Grievance collecting:* Keeping track of everything anyone has ever done to hurt or disappoint you and letting that person hear about it is another way of ex- pressing envy. Grievance collectors are convinced that life treats them unfairly, and they keep mental records to prove it.

We all act on, rather than acknowledge and tolerate, our envy at one time or another. By becoming aware of

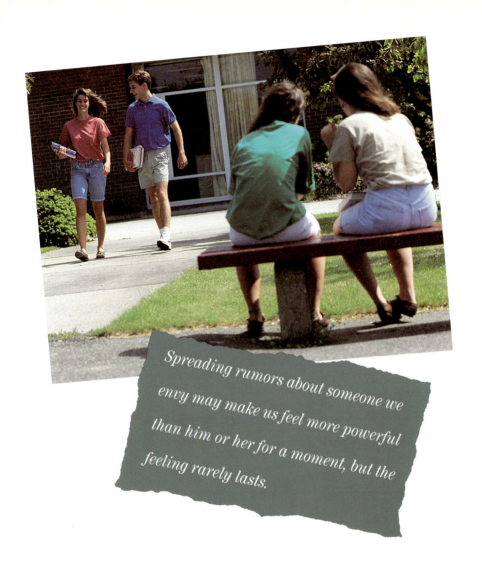

Spreading rumors about someone we envy may make us feel more powerful than him or her for a moment, but the feeling rarely lasts.

our own envy habits, we can catch ourselves in the act. Then we can decide what to do with our envy. This awareness brings power. It leads us to many new routes for acquiring love, which is what we're really after. With awareness, we can control our envy rather than letting it control us.

Take Charge!
Know Your Envy Habits

Read each of the following statements. Try to think of a time when you felt what the statement expresses. If something comes to mind, write down what happened and how you felt about it. The feeling may have passed in a flash or stayed with you for a while. Make a note of this, too. Can you think of other times you felt the same way?

1. Sometimes I want something that someone else has so badly that I hate them for having it.

2. I feel upset instead of happy when friends or siblings get something they really want. I find it hard to join in their pleasure and say something nice.

3. Sometimes I feel glad instead of sorry when friends or siblings don't get what they want.

4. I feel a flash of anger when someone else gets a compliment.

5. No matter how hard I try, I can't compliment someone sincerely.

6. If I can't have something I want, I'll make sure no one can have it.

7. If someone else succeeds, I can't.

8. Sometimes I spread rumors about someone who is popular or successful, even though I know the information isn't true.

9. Sometimes I put people down — even people I secretly admire.

10. I always remember when someone wrongs me.

11. I feel like I never have enough, no matter how much I have.

Read your notes when you've finished. What are your envy habits? Remember, envy is neither good nor bad. We all feel it and we all sometimes act badly because of it. The intent of this exercise is to help you identify the ways you typically express envy so that you can gain better control over the feeling.

Write down what happened and how you felt about it. The feeling may have passed in a flash or stayed with you for a while. Make a note of this, too.

A Tale of Two Friends

A woman named Nadine remembers a good friend she lost in junior high because of envy.

"Lesley and I were best friends," Nadine recalls. "We did everything together. Most of all, we dreamed about what life would be like once we were movie stars. Then, in eighth grade, our school put on a play. We both tried out for the lead. We promised we'd be happy no matter who got the part, but it didn't work out that way. She got it, and I was *not* happy. But I couldn't admit this, not even to myself.

"At first, I acted as if nothing had changed. But then I started complaining to Lesley that she never spent time with me any more because she was too busy rehearsing. She argued that whenever she called me, *I* was the one too busy to talk. Of course, she was right. When Lesley got the part, I suddenly got very 'busy' shopping at the mall and hanging out with my other friends.

"But that wasn't the worst of it," Nadine

continues. "I started acting on my envy, telling people that the only reason Lesley got the part was because she flirted with the drama coach. Pretty soon, a rumor was spreading that she and the coach had a thing going. Of course this wasn't true, but I said nothing to stop it. When Lesley found out how the rumor got started, she was furious. She stopped speaking to me. Looking back, I can see that I was so envious of Lesley that I was willing to ruin our friendship just to hurt her and reduce her success. I felt hurt inside but couldn't face it head on. How awful for both of us!"

As Nadine's experience painfully demonstrates, envy can ruin relationships. It can hurt both the person envied and the envier. But it doesn't have to. Had Nadine been able to recognize, understand, and share her feelings, perhaps she and Lesley could have worked things out. Perhaps Nadine could have found a way to share the excitement of the school play — by volunteering to help with costumes or makeup, for example. Perhaps she could have helped Lesley work on her part, watching what her friend did so that she could learn and do better herself at a future tryout. Perhaps she could have asked the drama coach to recommend an acting teacher. Had Nadine been able to be aware of and share her envious feelings, she would have had many choices about what to do. Instead, she had none. Her envy ruled her behavior.

Envy and Friendship

Envy between friends is normal. We constantly compare ourselves to others. And we compare ourselves most to the people closest to us. Our friends are often the yardstick by which we measure our own successes and failures. Sometimes we think we come up short. Then we may feel envy. Certain common situations heighten envy. Chief among them are the following:

■ *Competition:* Nadine and Lesley couldn't both win the lead in the play. One of them had to lose, and the loser was bound to feel bad. Feeling envious in such a situation is natural. Nadine and Lesley were fooling themselves when they thought that their friendship could overcome this very normal reaction. However, as Nadine later realized, she did have a choice about how she expressed her envy.

■ *Loss:* The feelings that follow a major loss can include envy of those who still have what one has lost. A friend whose parents divorce may envy one whose family is still together. One who is fired from a part-time job may envy a friend who is still working.

■ *Love:* When a friend falls in love, we sometimes feel jealous of the romantic partner and envious of the time and gifts and attention our friend now gives the girlfriend or boyfriend. **Jealousy** and envy are similar emotions, but they are not the same. They often come at the same time, however. We feel jealous when we are afraid of losing something we have — a friendship, for example. We feel envious of things we do not have and believe we will never get — the gifts or trips to the beach our friend is sharing with his or her partner. Jealousy is usually not as strongly felt as envy.

■ *Change in status:* Any change in status, which is the position of one friend relative to the other, can cause envy. Friends who were equal suddenly aren't. Losses and love can both bring changes in status. So can many other things. One friend may make the team he tries out for while the other doesn't, for example, or only one might be accepted in the "popular" crowd. Since our opportunities and relationships change often, so does our status relative to our friends and others.

Envy may be an inevitable part of friendship, but the hurt envy can cause need not be. Friends can work out their envious feelings. When they do, their friendship can become stronger. They will learn that it can survive an envy attack.

Take Charge!
Clear the Air About Envy

Many times, the best way for friends to resolve envy is to talk about it. This goes for the person who is envied as well as the one who is doing the envying. Being envied can hurt as much as feeling envy. An envied person may not understand why a good friend is staying away or being mean. He or she may feel cheated out of the pleasure of sharing good news if the friend reacts badly. The envied friend may even put off telling or, worse, cover up a success out of fear of arousing envy. Jeff, for example, was excited about being selected for the school chorus until he thought about Matt.

"Matt's a good friend," Jeff says, "but I always feel uncomfortable telling him when something really great's happened. He'll say he's happy for me, but I can tell he's really not. And then after, it's like he's really distant for a while. You know, too busy to get together when

I call, that kind of stuff. When I got chosen for the chorus, I decided not to tell him right away. What a mistake! He heard from someone else, and that made it worse."

Matt and Jeff might be able to keep envy from further hurting their friendship if they talk things through. So might you if you have an envy problem with a friend — or with anyone else, for that matter. Here are some techniques that can help you share your feelings in a way that will encourage the other person to listen.

■ Tell your friend that you value the friendship and don't want to lose it, but you are having a hard time right now. Then tell about *your* feelings. For example, Matt might tell Jeff, "When I got chosen for the chorus I felt really happy, but I didn't tell you because I was afraid you'd pull away from me, like what happened when I got to go on the band trip to Florida and you didn't." Take the risk for the sake of the friendship.

■ Search for the need or wish behind your envy. As you know, envious feelings are usually a signal that something deeper is missing. Ask yourself, "What do I think the thing I envy will get me? What do I really want?" If you can, express the deeper wishes and hopes.

■ Use **"I" statements** and a calm tone of voice. Such statements express how you feel without blaming or attacking your friend. Compare these two comments: (in a calm, maybe hurt, tone) "I guess I wish I'd gotten the

Many times, the best way to resolve envy is to talk about it. This is true whether you are the envious one or the target of envy.

part in the play. I've envied you ever since you did, and it doesn't feel good" and (in an angry tone) "You're really rubbing it in my face about the play. How could I not feel envious?" Which would you rather hear?

■ Try **active listening**. When you use this technique, you listen without interrupting and repeat to yourself what the other person is saying even when you disagree. This gives your friend a chance to share feelings, too. By listening — really listening — to each other, you and your friend will better understand each other's needs and **vulnerabilities**. You'll learn to tolerate the fact that you may have different memories or views of what happened. Don't argue the facts. Talk about feelings. Sometimes, feeling understood is enough to make you feel better even if nothing changes.

■ If you are the envier, ask your friend what he or she envies in you. You might be surprised to learn that you have traits or accomplishments someone else might want! And if you are the one who is envied, tell your friend what you envy in him or her. This puts some equality back into the relationship. It can also make your friend feel more valuable.

If envy is leading you to do destructive things, or if you always feel envious of someone, consider talking with a therapist.

What if Talking Doesn't Work?

There's no guarantee that talking will sap envy of its destructive power. Some people simply cannot face envy in themselves. Others are not willing to let go of it. If you are the object of envy, you may be unable to save the friendship. Or you may need to decide whether you are willing to live with your friend's envy. We often reach a point in our relationships when we see things we don't like in the other person — or in ourselves. When this happens, we need to weigh the bad and the good.

Sometimes the price we pay for a friend's envy is pretty high. If you find yourself hiding your successes, lying about them, or limiting your own opportunities so that you don't make a friend envious, you may be paying too high a price. Tell your friend what you're feeling. If things don't get better after you talk, you may need to consider whether the friendship should continue. If the person who envies you is a family member, you have a more difficult problem. Talking to a third party may help. A parent or grandparent, for example, may be able to help resolve problems between siblings.

A third party may also be able to help you deal with your own envy. A trusted adult might be able to help you better understand your feelings and what they are telling you. Understanding is the first step in figuring out what you need to meet your needs. And meeting your needs loosens the grip of envy.

If envy is leading you to do destructive things, or if you *always* feel envious of someone, consider talking with a therapist. You shouldn't have to live with the pain, unhappiness, and broken relationships that constant envying brings. You deserve better!

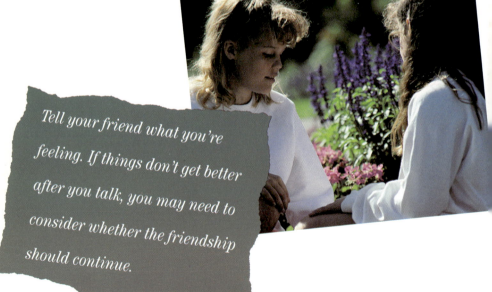

Tell your friend what you're feeling. If things don't get better after you talk, you may need to consider whether the friendship should continue.

A Final Word

You've learned in this book that envy can be a teacher. It can broaden our awareness and the choices we have in our lives. Envy directs our attention to needs and desires we may not have known we had or may have only partly met. In the teen years, when we are struggling with the issues of who we are and who we want to be, envy can be particularly useful. It can help point the way to answers.

As we answer the questions about our own identities, becoming more secure about who we are and our place in the world, we can move from envy to admiration. We can take pride in our friends' and family's successes as well as in our own. We can see that our friends' triumphs are our triumphs, too. When the people we care about feel good about themselves, they are better able to give to and support us and our successes.

When we feel the flash of envy, we can recognize it for what it is: one inner voice

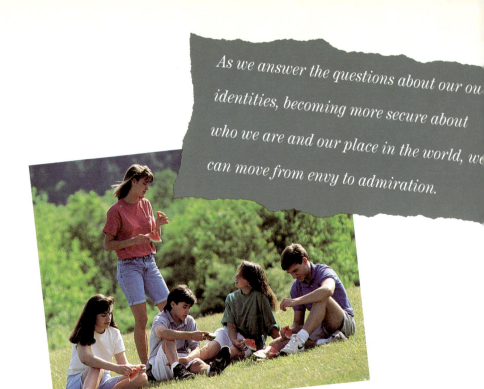

As we answer the questions about our ou
identities, becoming more secure about
who we are and our place in the world, we
can move from envy to admiration.

among many, there to help us better know ourselves. We
can welcome it. We can sit back and say, "Okay. What do
you have to teach me today?" The needs and wishes
behind our envy are the building blocks of our dreams.
They help us recover parts of ourselves we buried and
lost in earlier years. By attending to these needs and
wishes, by viewing the people we envy as models rather
than rivals, we can begin putting the building blocks
together. We can work toward realizing the dream of
what we want our lives to be.

If You'd Like to Learn More

Books and Movies

Books and movies can help us understand our emotions better. Here are some that deal with envy.

Blubber by Judy Blume (New York: Bradbury Press, 1974). When Linda, an overweight girl in the fifth grade, is tormented and nicknamed "Blubber," she longs to be treated like a normal kid and accepted by her classmates.

We Lived in the Almont by Eleanor Clymer (New York: E.P. Dutton & Co., 1970). Linda Martin is happily living in the Almont, an old building where her hard-working but poor father is the super. But when she learns that her friend Sharon Ross lives in a luxury apartment house with lots of great stuff, Linda becomes envious of her friend's comfortable life.

And Philippa Makes Four by Martha Derman (New York: Four Winds Press, 1983). When Philippa's widowed father falls in love with the divorced mother of her school enemy, Libby, Philippa finds herself envious of the love that her father is sharing with these new people in his life.

One Thing for Sure by David Gifaldi (New York: Clarion Books, 1986). Twelve-year-old Dylan has a father who is serving time in prison and a group of former friends who constantly remind him about his father's crime. He longs to have a normal family life, escape his father's shadow, and win acceptance for being himself.

Amadeus (1984). Envy is at the heart of this Oscar-winning film about the musical genius Wolfgang Amadeus Mozart. An envious rival ruins Mozart's life, eventually causing his death.

David Copperfield (1935). This movie classic is based on a book by Charles Dickens. It traces the adventures of David Copperfield as he grows to manhood, including his encounters with the envious Uriah Heep.

Glossary/Index

active listening: 41 The technique of concentrating on what someone is saying without interrupting.

analyst: 12 Someone who is trained in a specific school of psychotherapy called psychoanalysis, and who studies experiences that are usually linked to early childhood.

culture: 21 The customs and beliefs that characterize a society or a part of a society.

disowned selves: 15 Those personality traits that have been buried because one learned early in life that they would not help get one's needs met.

envy: 5 The uncomfortable feeling of wanting something someone else has so badly that it hurts and believing that one will never get it.

"I" statements: 39 Expressions of feelings that start with the word *I*. They state what the speaker is feeling without attacking the listener.

jealousy: 37 Fear of losing what one has, especially the love or affection of another. Jealousy often feels less intense and is more easily acknowledged than envy.

peer group: 21 Classmates and others one's own age.

primary selves: 15 The parts of one's personality that worked in early childhood to get one's needs filled and thus became one's defining traits.

psychiatrist: 12 A medical doctor who studies how people feel, act, and think, and who treats people who are emotionally troubled.

psychologist: 15 A person trained to understand human behavior and emotions and to help those who are emotionally troubled.

sibling rivalry: 12 The normal envy between brothers and sisters.

temperament: 14 The set of emotional responses that is characteristic of a given individual.

vulnerabilities: 41 Doubts about oneself that leave one open to being emotionally hurt.